THOMAS KINSELLA

Fifteen Dead

THE DOLMEN PRESS
in association with
OXFORD UNIVERSITY PRESS
1979

*Set in Baskerville type
and printed and published in the Republic of Ireland
at the Dolmen Press
North Richmond Street, Dublin 1
in association with
Oxford University Press*

OXFORD LONDON GLASGOW
NEW YORK   TORONTO   MELBOURNE   WELLINGTON
KUALA LUMPUR   SINGAPORE   JAKARTA   HONG KONG   TOKYO
DELHI   BOMBAY   CALCUTTA   MADRAS   KARACHI
IBADAN   NAIROBI   DAR ES SALAAM   CAPE TOWN

Designed by Liam Miller

*

First published 1979

ISBN 0 85105 328 9 THE DOLMEN PRESS
ISBN 0 19 211890 0 OXFORD UNIVERSITY PRESS

© 1972, 1973, 1974, 1979 *Thomas Kinsella*

by THOMAS KINSELLA

poetry

SELECTED POEMS

NEW POEMS 1973

ONE AND OTHER POEMS

*

THE TAIN

CONTENTS

TO LIAM MILLER
FOR ALL HIS GENEROSITY

Peppercanister was established in 1972 as a small private publishing enterprise, with the purpose of issuing occasional special items from our home in Dublin, across the Grand Canal from St. Stephen's Church, known locally as 'The Peppercanister'.

Peppercanister is a development of a long-standing relationship with the Dolmen Press. The main idea was to publish fine books in the form and materials most suitable to the longer poems and sequences I had started writing, in the limited editions which are enough to satisfy the market for such books. These first editions would constitute an interim form of publication, and would be collected when appropriate in ordinary trade editions.

The idea was amended in practice : *Butcher's Dozen*, the first publication, was printed hurriedly in large quantities as a cheap pamphlet, with the special bound edition almost as an afterthought. *A Selected Life*, the second publication, was published primarily in pamphlet form also, as a fund-raising scheme for Fundúireacht an Riadaigh, the Seán O Riada Memorial Foundation. Subsequent *Peppercanister* publications have followed the same pattern — small pamphlet editions subsidised, in effect, by the specials.

Butcher's Dozen was published in April 1972, a week after the Report of the Widgery Tribunal of Inquiry into the shooting of thirteen Civil Rights demonstrators by the British army in Derry on 30 January. The poem was issued in an unlimited edition in wrappers and a signed and limited bound edition of 125 copies. Both editions were decorated with the badge issued at the Civil Rights protest march in Newry on 6 February 1972. There was a limited reissue in 1974 of 175 bound copies.

A Selected Life, published in July 1972, is a funeral poem written in memory of Seán O Riada, composer and musician, who died in October 1971. The poem was issued in an edition of 1,000 copies in wrappers and 150 copies signed and bound, and was decorated with a profile medallion of O Riada based on the death mask made by the sculptor Seamus Murphy.

Vertical Man was published in August 1973 in an edition of 350 copies in wrappers, with 100 signed and bound. The poem is a sequel to *A Selected Life* and is set in Philadelphia on the first anniversary of O Riada's death.

The Good Fight, a poem for the tenth anniversary of the death of John F. Kennedy, was published in November 1973 in an edition of 1,500 copies in wrappers and 125 copies signed and bound. The poem was decorated with a series of portrait heads of Plato.

These four occasional poems made up the first series of *Peppercanister* publications, and are collected in this volume with a commentary.

T. K.

BUTCHER'S DOZEN

1972

BUTCHER'S DOZEN:
A LESSON FOR
THE OCTAVE OF WIDGERY

I went with Anger at my heel
Through Bogside of the bitter zeal
— Jesus pity! — on a day
Of cold and drizzle and decay.
A month had passed. Yet there remained
A murder smell that stung and stained.
On flats and alleys — over all —
It hung; on battered roof and wall,
On wreck and rubbish scattered thick,
On sullen steps and pitted brick.
And when I came where thirteen died
It shrivelled up my heart. I sighed
And looked about that brutal place
Of rage and terror and disgrace.
Then my moistened lips grew dry.
I had heard an answering sigh!
There in a ghostly pool of blood
A crumpled phantom hugged the mud:
'Once there lived a hooligan.
A pig came up, and away he ran.
Here lies one in blood and bones,
Who lost his life for throwing stones.'
More voices rose. I turned and saw
Three corpses forming, red and raw,
From dirt and stone. Each upturned face
Stared unseeing from its place:
'Behind this barrier, blighters three,
We scrambled back and made to flee.
The guns cried *Stop*, and here lie we.'

[13]

Then from left and right they came,
More mangled corpses, bleeding, lame,
Holding their wounds. They chose their ground,
Ghost by ghost, without a sound,
And one stepped forward, soiled and white :
'A bomber I. I travelled light
— Four pounds of nails and gelignite
About my person, hid so well
They seemed to vanish where I fell.
When the bullet stopped my breath
A doctor sought the cause of death.
He upped my shirt, undid my fly,
Twice he moved my limbs awry,
And noticed nothing. By and by
A soldier, with his sharper eye,
Beheld the four elusive rockets
Stuffed in my coat and trouser pockets.
Yes, they must be strict with us,
Even in death so treacherous !'
He faded, and another said :
'We three met close when we were dead.
Into an armoured car they piled us
Where our mingled blood defiled us,
Certain, if not dead before,
To suffocate upon the floor.
Careful bullets in the back
Stopped our terrorist attack,
And so three dangerous lives are done
— Judged, condemned and shamed in one.'
That spectre faded in his turn.
A harsher stirred, and spoke in scorn :
'The shame is theirs, in word and deed,
Who prate of Justice, practise greed,

And act in ignorant fury — then,
Officers and gentlemen,
Send to their Courts for the Most High
To tell us did we really die!
Does it need recourse to law
To tell ten thousand what they saw?
Law that lets them, caught red-handed,
Halt the game and leave it stranded,
Summon up a sworn inquiry
And dump their conscience in the diary.
During which hiatus, should
Their legal basis vanish, good,
The thing is rapidly arranged :
Where's the law that can't be changed?
The news is out. The troops were kind.
Impartial justice has to find
We'd be alive and well today
If we had let them have their way.
Yet England, even as you lie,
You give the facts that you deny.
Spread the lie with all your power
— All that's left; it's turning sour.
Friend and stranger, bride and brother,
Son and sister, father, mother,
All not blinded by your smoke,
Photographers who caught your stroke,
The priests that blessed our bodies, spoke
And wagged our blood in the world's face.
The truth will out, to your disgrace.'
He flushed and faded. Pale and grim,
A joking spectre followed him :
'Take a bunch of stunted shoots,
A tangle of transplanted roots,

Ropes and rifles, feathered nests,
Some dried colonial interests,
A hard unnatural union grown
In a bed of blood and bone,
Tongue of serpent, gut of hog
Spiced with spleen of underdog.
Stir in, with oaths of loyalty,
Sectarian supremacy,
And heat, to make a proper botch,
In a bouillon of bitter Scotch.
Last, the choice ingredient : you.
Now, to crown your Irish stew,
Boil it over, make a mess.
A most imperial success !'
He capered weakly, racked with pain,
His dead hair plastered in the rain :
The group was silent once again.
It seemed the moment to explain
That sympathetic politicians
Say our violent traditions,
Backward looks and bitterness
Keep us in this dire distress.
We must forget, and look ahead,
Nurse the living, not the dead.
My words died out. A phantom said :
'Here lies one who breathed his last
Firmly reminded of the past.
A trooper did it, on one knee,
In tones of brute authority.'
That harsher spirit, who before
Had flushed with anger, spoke once more :
'Simple lessons cut most deep.
This lesson in our hearts we keep :

[16]

Persuasion, protest, arguments,
The milder forms of violence,
Earn nothing but polite neglect.
England, the way to your respect
Is via murderous force, it seems;
You push us to your own extremes.
You condescend to hear us speak
Only when we slap your cheek.
And yet we lack the last technique :
We rap for order with a gun,
The issues simplify to one
— Then your Democracy insists
You mustn't talk with terrorists !
White and yellow, black and blue,
Have learnt their history from you :
Divide and ruin, muddle through,
Not principled, but politic.
— In strength, perfidious; weak, a trick
To make good men a trifle sick.
We speak in wounds. Behold this mess.
My curse upon your politesse.'
Another ghost stood forth, and wet
Dead lips that had not spoken yet :
'My curse on the cunning and the bland,
On gentlemen who loot a land
They do not care to understand;
Who keep the natives on their paws
With ready lash and rotten laws;
Then if the beasts erupt in rage
Give them a slightly larger cage
And, in scorn and fear combined,
Turn them against their own kind.
The game runs out of room at last,

[17]

A people rises from its past,
The going gets unduly tough
And you have (surely . . . ?) had enough.
The time has come to yield your place
With condescending show of grace
— An Empire-builder handing on.
We reap the ruin when you've gone,
All your errors heaped behind you :
Promises that do not bind you,
Hopes in conflict, cramped commissions,
Faiths exploited, and traditions.'
Bloody sputum filled his throat,
He stopped and coughed to clear it out,
And finished, with his eyes a-glow :
'You came, you saw, you conquered . . . So.
You gorged — and it was time to go.
Good riddance. We'd forget — released —
But for the rubbish of your feast,
The slops and scraps that fell to earth
And sprang to arms in dragon birth.
Sashed and bowler-hatted, glum
Apprentices of fife and drum,
High and dry, abandoned guards
Of dismal streets and empty yards,
Drilled at the codeword "True Religion"
To strut and mutter like a pigeon
"Not An Inch — Up The Queen";
Who use their walls like a latrine
For scribbled magic — at their call,
Straight from the nearest music-hall,
Pope and Devil intertwine,
Two cardboard kings appear, and join
In one more battle by the Boyne !

Who could love them? God above. . .'
'Yet pity is akin to love,'
The thirteenth corpse beside him said,
Smiling in its bloody head,
'And though there's reason for alarm
In dourness and a lack of charm
Their cursed plight calls out for patience.
They, even they, with other nations
Have a place, if we can find it.
Love our changeling! Guard and mind it.
Doomed from birth, a cursed heir,
Theirs is the hardest lot to bear,
Yet not impossible, I swear,
If England would but clear the air
And brood at home on her disgrace
— Everything to its own place.
Face their walls of dole and fear
And be of reasonable cheer.
Good men every day inherit
Father's foulness with the spirit,
Purge the filth and do not stir it.
Let them out! At least let in
A breath or two of oxygen,
So they may settle down for good
And mix themselves in the common blood.
We all are what we are, and that
Is mongrel pure. What nation's not
Where any stranger hung his hat
And seized a lover where she sat?'
He ceased and faded. Zephyr blew
And all the others faded too.
I stood like a ghost. My fingers strayed
Along the fatal barricade.

[19]

The gentle rainfall drifting down
Over Colmcille's town
Could not refresh, only distil
In silent grief from hill to hill.

A SELECTED LIFE

&

VERTICAL MAN

1972   1973

A SELECTED LIFE

I

Galloping Green: May 1962

HE clutched the shallow drum
and crouched forward, thin
as a beast of prey. The shirt
stretched at his waist. He stared
to one side, toward the others,
and struck the skin cruelly
with his nails. Sharp
as the answering arid bark
his head quivered, counting.

2

Coolea: 6 October 1971

A fine drizzle blew
softly across the tattered valley
onto my glasses, and covered
my mourning suit with tiny drops.

A crow scuffled in the hedge
and floated out with a dark groan
into full view. It flapped up the field
and lit on a rock, and scraped its beak.
It croaked : a voice out of the rock
carrying across the slope. Foretell.

Foretell : the Sullane river winding downward
in darker green through the fields
and disappearing behind his house;
cars parking in the lane; a bare yard;
family and friends collecting in the kitchen;
a shelf there, concertinas sprawled in the dust,
the pipes folded on their bag.
The hole waiting in the next valley.
That.

A rat lay on its side in the wet,
the grey skin washed clean and fleshy,
the little face wrinkled back in hatred,
the back torn open. A pale string
stretched on the gravel. Devil-martyr;
your sad, mad meat. . .
                        I have interrupted
some thing . . . You! Croaking
on your wet stone. Flesh picker.

The drizzle came thick and fast suddenly.
Down in the village the funeral bell began to beat.

*

And you. Waiting in the dark chapel.
Packed and ready. Upon your hour.
Leaving. . . A few essentials forgotten

— a standard array of dependent beings,
small, smaller, pale, paler, in black;

[24]

— sundry musical effects : a piercing
sweet consort of whistles crying,
goosenecked wail and yelp of pipes,
melodeons snoring in sadness,
drum bark, the stricken
harpsichord's soft crash;

— a lurid cabinet : fire's flames
plotting in the dark; hugger mugger
and murder; collapsing back in laughter.
Angry goblets of Ireland's tears,
stuffed with fire, touch. Salut!
Men's guts ignite and whiten in satisfaction;

— a workroom, askew : fumbling at the table
tittering, pools of idea forming.
A contralto fills the room
with Earth's autumnal angst; the pools coalesce.
Here and there in the shallows dim spirits
glide, poissons de la melancolie.
The banks above are smothered in roses;
among their glowing harmonies, bathed in charm,
a cavalier retires in fancy dress,
embracing her loving prize; two baby angels,
each holding a tasseled curtain-corner,
flutter down, clucking and mocking complacently.
Liquids of romance, babbling
on the concrete floor. Let us draw a veil. . .

3

St. Gobnait's Graveyard, Ballyvourney:
that evening

THE gate creaked in the dusk. The trampled grass,
  soaked and still, was disentangling
among the standing stones
after the day's excess.

A flock of crows circled
the church tower, scattered
and dissolved chattering
into the trees.   Fed.

His first buried night
drew on.   Unshuddering.
And welcome . . .
Shudder for him,

Pierrot limping forward in the sun
out of Merrion Square, long ago,
in black overcoat and beret,
pale as death from his soiled bed,

swallowed back : animus
brewed in clay, uttered
in brief meat and brains, flattened
back under our flowers.

Gold and still he lay,
on his secondlast bed. *Dottore!* A withered smile,
the wry hands lifted. *A little while
and you may not. . .*

Salut.
Slán.
Yob tvoyu mat'.
Master, your health.

4

Philadelphia: 3 October 1972

I was pouring a drink when the night-monotony
was startled below by a sudden howling
of engines along Market Street,
curséd ambulances intermixing their screams
down the dark canyons.

Over the gramophone your death-mask
was suddenly awake
and I felt something of you
out in the night, near and moving nearer,
tittering, uneasy.

I thought we had laid you to rest
— that you had been directed toward
crumbling silence, and the like.
It seems it is hard to keep
a vertical man down.

I lifted the glass, and the furies
redoubled their distant screams.
To you : the bourbon-breath.
To me, for the time being,
the real thing. . .

'THERE has grown lately upon the soul
        a covering as of earth and stone,
thick and rough . . .'
                    I had been remembering
the sour ancient phrases . . .
                            'Very well,
seemingly the argument requires it :
let us assume mankind is worth considering . . .'

That particular heaviness.

                        That the days pass,
that our tasks arise, dominate our energies,
are mastered with difficulty and some pleasure,
and are obsolete. That there can be a sweet stir
hurrying in the veins (earned : this sunlight
— this oxygen — are my *reward* !) and the ground
grows dull to the tread. The ugly rack : let it ride.
That you may startle the heart of a whole people
(as you know) and all your power,
with its delicate, self-mocking adjustments,
is soon beating to a coarse pulse
to glut fantasy and sentiment.
That for all you have done, the next beginning
is as lonely, as random, as gauche and unready,
as presumptuous, as the first,
when you stripped and advanced timidly
toward nothing in particular.
Though with a difference — there is
a kind of residue. Not an increase in weight
(we must not become portly; your admired D******,
the lush intellectual glamour loosening
to reveal the travelogue beneath).

But a residue in the timidity,
a maturer unsureness, as we
prepare to undergo preparatory error.

ONLY this morning . . . that desultory moment or two
standing at the rain-stained glass; a while more
looking over the charts pinned on the wall;
to sit down with the folder of notes on the left
and clean paper on the right, the pen beside it,
and remove and put down the spectacles and bury
my face in my hands, in self-devouring prayer,
till the charts and notes come crawling to life again
under a Night seething with
soft incandescent bombardment!

At the dark zenith a pulse beat,
a sperm of light separated wriggling
and snaked in a slow beam down
the curve of the sky, through faint
structures and hierarchies
of elements and things and beasts. It fell,
a packed star, dividing
and redividing until it was
a multiple gold tear. It dropped
toward the horizon, entered
bright Quincunx newly risen,
beat with a blinding flame and dis-
appeared. I stared, duly blinded.
An image burned on the brain
— a woman-animal : scaled,
pierced in paws and heart,
ecstatically calm. It faded
to a far-off desolate call,

                    a child's . . .

If the eye could follow that, accustomed to
that dark . . .
            But that is your domain.

A T which thought, your presence
   turned back toward the night.
                        (*Wohin . . .*)
                                        Stay
a while. Since you are here.
                        At least
we have *Das Lied von der Erde*
and a decent record-player together
at the one place and time.
                        With a contraction
of the flesh . . . A year exactly since you died !

I arrested the needle. The room filled
with a great sigh. In terror and memory
I lowered the tiny point toward our youth
— into those bright cascades !
                        Radiant outcry —
trumpets and drenching strings — exultant tenor —
Schadenfreude! The waste !
                        Abject. Irrecoverable . . .

                        *

T HE golden bourbon winks in the glass. For the road.
   But wait, there is something I must show you first,
a song of cark and care. A drinking — a *drunken* — song
for the misery of this world. . . Not quite right yet
— but very soulful. To give you a hollow laugh.

Let Gloom gather, and deject
    the soul's gardens.
Let Joy shrivel up and die
    and song with it.
For Life is a black business.
    While as for Death —

Therefore, a little music, a little something
    — a timely tumbler.
Earth has not anything
    to show more fair,
Life being what it is.
    And as for Death —

The azure firmament
    is permanent.
The Earth is here to stay
    and always good
for another Primavera.
    Whereas Man —

Would you care to share a queer vision I had?
By your gravestone. . .
                        It was moonlight.
And there was something crouching there —
    ape-shaped ! —
demented, howling out
silent foulness, accurséd silent screams
into the fragrant Night . . .

THE golden goodness trembles. It is time.
And more than time. Kindly
step forward.
                    A black
bloody business,
                    the whole thing . . .

He stepped forward through the cigarette-smoke
to his place at the piano
— all irritation — and tore
off his long fingernails to play.

From palatal darkness a voice
rose flickering, and checked
in glottal silence. The song
articulated and pierced.

We leaned over the shallows from the boat slip
and netted the little grey shrimp-ghosts
snapping, and dropped them
in the crawling biscuit-tin.

THE GOOD FIGHT
A POEM FOR THE TENTH ANNIVERSARY
OF THE DEATH OF
JOHN F. KENNEDY

1973

In 1962 . . . people began seriously to calculate that, if the three brothers took the Presidency in succession, it would carry the country to 1984 . . . the succession could then pass to the sons.

Henry Fairlie, *The Kennedy Promise*, London, 1973.

Those who are imprisoned in the silence of reality always use a gun (or, if they are more fortunate, a pen) to speak for them.

John Clellon Holmes, 'The Silence of Oswald', *Playboy*, November 1965.

No sir, I killed nobody.

Lee Harvey Oswald, Dallas Police Headquarters, 22 November 1963.

THE GOOD FIGHT

I

ONCE upon a time a certain phantom
took to certain red-smelling corridors
in sore need. It met, with a flush of pleasure,
the smell of seed and swallowed
life and doom in the same animal action.

(Mere substance — our metier.
This is our nature, the human mouth
tasting Justice or a favourite soup
with equal relish.)

He wiped his lips
and leaned tiredly against the window,
flying through the night. The darkened cabin
creaked under a few weak blue lights.
Outside, half seen, the fields of stars
chilled his forehead, their millions centred on
the navigator.
Not commanding. Steering.

Can we believe it possible for anyone
to master the art of steering while he must
at the same time expend his best skill
gaining control of the helm?

His hands flexed.
All reasonable things are possible.

All that day, the reporters in the corridor
had pushed closer to the room.
As the hours passed, the press of human beings
— the sweat and smoke — built up
a meaty odour.

Once, he rolled up his sleeve
and looked at the calloused, scratched arm :
'Ohio did that to me.'
(One day in Philadelphia
his hand *burst* with blood.)

He rolled the sleeve down again
and shook his head, not understanding,
then became cool again as ever,
asking : 'Who made that decision?
Who had command decision then?'

*

Shock-headed, light-footed, he swung
an invisible cloak about him in the uproar
and hunched down from the platform at them,
his hands in his jacket pockets.
A jugular pleasure beat in his throat.

'Ever free and strong
we will march along, going to meet
the harsh bright demands of the West, building
a new City on a New Frontier,
where led and leader bend their wills together
in necessary rule — admit
no limit but the possible, grant

[38]

to each endeavour its appointed post,
its opportunity to serve :
our Youth carrying its ideals
into the fettered places of the earth;
our Strength on guard at every door of freedom
around the world; our Art and Music
down from the dark garret — into the sun !
The eyes of the world upon us !'

He held out his inflamed right hand
for the Jaw to grip. The sinews winced.
Crude hand-lettered signs danced in the murk.

'Forward, then, in higher urgency,
adventuring with risk,
raising each other to our moral best,
aspiring to the sublime
in warlike simplicity, our power
justified upon our excellence !

If other nations falter
their people still remain what they were.
But if our country in its call to greatness
falters, we are little but the scum
of other lands. That is our special danger,
our burden and our glory.
The accident that brought our people together
out of blind necessities
— embrace it ! — explosive — to our bodies.'

(It sounds as though it could go on for ever,
yet there is a shape to it — Appropriate
Performance. Another almost perfect
working model. . . But it gets harder.
The concepts jerk and wrestle, back to back.

[39]

The finer the idea the harder it is
to assemble lifelike. It adopts hardnesses
and inflexibilities, knots, impossible joints
made possible only by stress,
and good for very little afterward.)

'Welcome challenge, that can stretch
the two sinews of the Soul,
Body and Mind, to a pure pitch,
so we may strike the just note
inside and out. . .'

                  'Peace — a process,
a way of solving problems. . .'
                        'Leisure —
an opportunity to perfect
those things of which we now despair. . .'

' — Let us make ourselves vessels of decision !
We are not here to curse the darkness.
The old order changes ! Men
firm in purpose and clear in thought
channel by their own decisions
forces greater than any man !'

The swaying mass exclaimed
about the great
dream
        steps. . .

(*Where is a young man's heart in such a scene?*
Who would not be stunned by the beast's opinion?
Nor think wisdom control of the beast's moods?

What schooling will resist, and not be swamped
and swept downstream? What can a young man do?
Especially if he belong to a great city
and be one of her rich and noble citizens
and also fine to look upon, and tall?)

He turned to go, murmuring aside
with a boyish grin :
                              'If anybody calls
say I am
raping the intellectuals !'

Inside, a group of specialists,
chosen for their incomparable dash,
were gathered around
a map of the world's regions
with all kinds of precision instruments.

II

A lonely room.
                    An electric fire
glowing in one corner. He is lying on his side.
It is late. He is at the centre of a city,
awake.

          Above and below him
there are other rooms, with others in them.
He knows nobody as yet, and has
no wish to. Outside the window
the street noises ascend.

His cell hangs in the night.

He could give up.
But there is something he must do.

And though the night passes, and the morning
brings back familiarity, and he goes out
about his business as though nothing had changed
— energyless at his assigned tasks —
and though the evening comes and he discovers
for the first time where to buy bread and tomatoes,
milk and meat, and climbs the dirty stairs
and takes possession for the second time,
and soon discovers how to light the gas
and where to put things, and where to sit
so he can read and eat at the same time,
and reads a long time
with the crumbs hardening and a tawny scum
shrinking on the cold tea, and finally
ventures out for his first night prowl
and takes possession of his neighbourhood,
learning at each turn, and turns for home,
and takes possession for the third time,
and reads, and later settles to sleep; and though
next morning he wakes up to a *routine*
for the first time, and goes to work,
repeats his necessary purchases
and manages the routine a little better,
with a less conscious effort; and night begins
to bring familiarity, and finds him
beginning to think at last
of what he is here for; and night follows night
and on a certain evening he puts aside

his cup and plate, and draws his journal to him
and revolves his pen meditatively. . .

I cannot reach or touch anything.
I cannot lay my hand with normal weight
on anything. It is either nothing
or too much.
          I have stood out
in the black rain and waited
and concentrated among
those over-lit ruins
irritable and hungry
and not known what city.

I have glided in loveless dream transit
over the shadowy sea floor,
satisfied in the knowledge
that if I once slacken in my savagery
I will drown.

I have watched my own
theatrical eyes narrow
and noted under what stress
and ceaseless changes of mind.
I have seen very few
cut so dull and driven a figure,
masked in scorn or abrupt
impulse, knowing content
nowhere.
        And I have forgotten
what rain and why I waited
what city from room to room
forgotten what father. . .

But not
what hunger as I move
toward some far sum-total,
attacked under others' eyes.

I have seen myself, a 'thing'
in my own eyes, lifting
my hand empty and opening
and closing my mouth
in senseless mimicry
and wondered why I am alive
or why a man can live in this way.

I believed once that silence
encloses each one of us.
Now, if that silence does not
enclose *each*, as I am led
more and more to understand
— so that I truly am cut off,
a 'thing' in their eyes also —
I can, if my daydreams are right,
decide to end it.

Soak wrist in cold water
to numb the pain.
Then slash my left wrist.
Then plunge wrist into bathtub of hot water.
Somewhere, a violin plays,
as I watch my life whirl away.
I think to myself 'How easy to Die'
and 'A Sweet Death', (to violins).

Or I might reach out and touch.
And he would turn this way
inquiring — Who was that!
What decision was this. . .

and not justice? | **An ambitious man, in a city where honour is the dominant principle, is soon broken upon the city as a ship is broken on a reef.**

Passion, ignorance and concupiscence are obscurities clouding the soul's natural judgment. They are the origin of crime.

yet more savage!
conveyed! | **There is none so small or so high but that he shall pay the fitting penalty, either in this world or in some yet more savage place whither he shall be conveyed. . .**

Great crimes, that sink into the abyss. . .

Images of evil in a foul pasture. . .

squat! | **— There are those, lower still, that seat Greed and Money on their throne, and make Reason and the Spirit squat on the floor under it. . .**

[45]

— Democracy cries out for
Tyranny; and the Tyrant becomes
a wolf instead of a man. . .

The rest! The whole
world but one! An
impossible logic-being.

— The rest damned to a constant
flux of pain and pleasure. They
struggle greedily for their
pleasures, and butt and kick with
horns and hoofs of iron.

```
            man       beast

          (d)amn

                      best

          mean
                        r i
          team        b a ns
                        ^ ^
          meat
```

I wonder what would
happen if somebody was
to stand up and say he
was utterly opposed not
only to the government
but to the people, to the
entire land and complete
foundations of his
society?

III

SHE was humming to herself
    among the heavy-scented magnolia bowers,
chic, with shining eyes, smiling at
Power and its attendant graces,
Aphrodite in Washington,

when all of a sudden a black
shadow or a black ruin
or a cliff of black
crossed at rigid speed
and spoiled everything.

Everybody started throwing themselves down
and picking themselves up and running
around the streets looking in each other's face
and saying 'Catastrophe' and weeping
and saying 'Well! That's that.'

For a few days great numbers of people
couldn't sleep, and lost appetite. Children experienced
alarm at the sight of their parents crying.
There were many who admitted
they expected the President's ghost to appear.

Various forms of castration dreads emerged,
probably out of fear of retribution
for unconscious parricidal wishes.
Anxiety was widespread, with apprehension
of worse things to come.

It was unhealthy — a distortion of normal attitudes.
Things had been exalted
altogether out of proportion. Afterward,
when the shock was over, matters settled down
with surprising swiftness, almost with relief :

shudder
and return
            — a fish, flung back,
that lay stunned, shuddered into consciousness,
and dived back into the depths.

And somewhere in some laughable echo-chamber, for ever,
a prayer came snarling through devilish electrical smoke,
and, blinded by the light reflecting from
the snow everywhere, Dr. Frost tottered forward
scratching his head, and opening his mouth :

IV

I am in disarray. Maybe if I
  were to fumble through my papers again. . .
I can no longer, in the face of so much
— so much. . .
            It is very hard.

I say this that you may know.

But there is nothing for it. On this
everything in me is agreed.

[48]

So, weak a thousand ways,
I have come, I have made toward this place,
among wells of profound energy
and monuments to power and tedium. . .
Not in judgment, and not
in acceptance either.
                              Uncertain.
For if all you wish to do
is curse the world and your place in it
— well then. . .
                    But some appetite
is not satisfied
with that, is dissatisfied unless —

The manipulation, the special pleading,
the cross-weaving of these
'vessels of decision',
the one so 'heroic',
the other so. . .
                    You have to
wear them down against each other
to get any purchase,
and then there is this
strain.
            That all *un*reasonable things
are possible. *Everything*
that can happen will happen. . .

My brothers, huddled in wait,
feeble warriors, self-chosen,
in our secondary world. . .
— who can't take our eyes off anything;
who harp on Love and Art and Truth too often :

[49]

it is appropriate for us
to proceed now and make our attempts
in private, to shuffle off and disappoint
Plato.

      (His 'philosophic nature'
— balance, you will remember;
apportionment, as between Mind and Body!
Harmony, and proper pitch!
The Dance!)

        Plump and faithless;
cut, as it were, in the sinews
of our souls; each other's worst company;
it is we, letting things *be*,
who might come at understanding.
That is the source of our patience.
Reliable first in the direction
and finally in the particulars of our response,
fumbling from doubt to doubt,
one day we might knock
our papers together, and elevate them
(with a certain self-abasement)
— their gleaming razors
mirroring a primary world
where power also is a source of patience
for a while before the just flesh
falls back in black dissolution in its box.

COMMENTARY

COMMENTARY

BUTCHER'S DOZEN

On the afternoon of Sunday 30 January 1972 the Dublin radio programme was interrupted by an announcement that there had been shooting at a Civil Rights demonstration in Derry, and that thirteen demonstrators had been killed by the British army. The BBC in London announced that gunmen had opened fire on the army and that bombers in the crowd had forced the troops to retaliate; there was a lot of specific detail, supplied by the army.

Official British versions of Irish events have a bad reputation — certainly in Ireland. They are meant for immediate consumption by an outside world that is ill-informed and not much concerned. It soon became clear, not least from adjustments to the official British version, that there had been a brutal and stupid massacre.* It was apparent that 'Bloody Sunday' required more than the first official response. The British Government announced the setting-up of a Tribunal of Inquiry under the Chairmanship of Lord Widgery, the Lord Chief Justice, to make a full investigation.

---

*This is not necessarily to say that it was not deliberate. Brigadier Frank Kitson in his book *Low Intensity Operations* (London 1971) in considering the army's possible contribution to combating non-violent civil action, recognises 'the simplest method of all, which is to suppress the movement by the ruthless application of naked force. . .' He acknowledges that 'although non-violent campaigns are particularly vulnerable to this sort of action, it is most unlikely that the British government, or indeed any Western government, would be politically able to operate on these lines even if it wanted to do so.' In official British thinking Northern Ireland could well constitute a special limbo in this regard, as it does in so many others.

There had been other killings in the North, but this was the first in the latest 'troubles' that involved the British army. The old combination of brutality and unruffled falsehood awoke a mass of dormant feelings in the Republic. In Dublin, thousands watched in fury and approval as the British Embassy in Merrion Square was burned down. A usually dispassionate and mocking acquaintance said : 'You forget sometimes that you hate the English.' On Sunday 6 February, one week after Bloody Sunday, thousands travelled North over the border to join a protest march in Newry, going stubbornly against the wishes of the Civil Rights organisers, who wanted no Southern Republicanism taking over their protest. The Southern contingent was careful not to offend; they were quiet and obedient, content to stare into British guns.

Witnesses before Lord Widgery included people who had been present at the demonstration, ballistics and explosives experts and the paratroopers who had done the shooting — in their case with a dreadful comedy, as they were bundled in and out of the building to give their orchestrated, anonymous testimony. Their evidence was not fully reported in British newspapers at the time, but it was published in great detail in Ireland, and accumulated into a clear indictment of the British troops and their officers. The Tribunal, after a brief consideration, exonerated the troops more or less, and managed to leave a suspicion of conspiracy and covert violence hanging over some of the victims. The Tribunal's Report was published for a few pence a copy; the evidence was published separately, at more than a hundred pounds. It is not surprising that the discrepancies between the evidence and the Tribunal's findings were not immediately obvious to the casual reader.

Samuel Dash, a Philadelphia lawyer who came to international attention shortly afterward, during the Watergate investigations, reported in detail on the Tribunal's performance for the International League for the Rights of Man in New York. In his opinion

[54]

The record of the Widgery Tribunal justifies a finding
that the 13 known civilian dead were unarmed when they
were killed on January 30 1972 in Londonderry, and that
they were shot either recklessly or deliberately by paratroopers of the First Battalion Parachute Regiment. . .

He concluded :

. . . an official inquiry which began with promise did
not fulfil that promise. . . There remains the unfinished
business to see that a full measure of justice is provided
for those who were killed and wounded, as well as their
families. Great Britain and the world cannot simply walk
away from 'Bloody Sunday'.*

But they have done so. The British Ambassador to Ireland
at the time, Sir John Peck, has recently published his reminis-
cences, dealing largely with his time in Dublin. For him the
major and most dangerous event of the time was the burning
of his Embassy in Dublin. He accepts the findings of the
Widgery Tribunal at face value. He would accept that Bloody
Sunday could have another construction put upon it, but only
in 'certain circles'. I was in Philadelphia on the first anniversary of Bloody Sunday; a local group picketed the BOAC office
on Kennedy Boulevard, having failed to solve the problem
of picketing the British Consulate on the fifteenth floor of a
nearby office block. The event was mentioned briefly on the
radio, with the explanation that on Bloody Sunday the pre-
vious year a gun battle had broken out in Londonderry
between the IRA and the British army and that thirteen IRA
gunmen had been killed. Explanatory matter of this kind is
supplied on request by the British Information Service in the
United States; where else would a harrassed news editor turn,

*Justice Denied: A Challenge to Lord Widgery's Report on 'Bloody Sunday'.
Published by the Defence and Education Fund of the International
League for the Rights of Man, 777 United Nations Plaza, New York.

reporting on the same day the return of American troops from Vietnam? There is no Irish news agency.

Foreign ignorance of Irish matters goes deep, even where there is general sympathy. I took a taxi to the Philadelphia Airport about this time and fell into conversation with the driver. Having discovered, without too much difficulty, that I was Irish, and travelling to Dublin, he told me (with all due consideration and courtesy, and making allowance for honourable exceptions) that he would be ashamed to be Irish. I asked him his origins : he was Scottish Presbyterian.

This is no place to 'set things straight'. The facts are available in any event in Liam de Paor's *Divided Ulster* (Penguin Books). And the point of view in *Butcher's Dozen* is clear enough. Though it was written in rage and haste at the time nothing has happened in the intervening six years that calls for serious revision (except possibly the 'happy ending').

Amid the swirling evils, miseries and stupidities in the North there are a few certainties :

(1) Northern Ireland is a state founded in injustice. It was established during a suspension of democratic process in Ireland — a suspension forced on the British Government by the Unionist minority. Its borders were fixed so as to contain the maximum area and resources over which that minority, on a return to democratic process, would remain a controlling majority.

(2) It is a state maintained in injustice, the artificially created minority North of the border being repressed and discriminated against for more than fifty years, while successive British Governments have ignored their responsibility in the matter.

(3) Withdrawal of the British army from Northern Ireland will not of itself solve anything. But no solution is possible without its withdrawal.

Violence is terrible, but it is not inhuman. In political terms it is the final response to unredressed injustice. And no amount of opposing violence will make it go away — only the removal of its causes. The British authorities have chosen, for passing expediencies in their own 'larger' politics, to evade the treatment of awkward, deep-seated causes in Ireland. This is nothing new on their part. But it was cause for great discouragement that politics in the Republic should have returned, under the Coalition Government of the middle 1970s, to a Redmondite posture, accommodating the British authorities in their evasion. Real issues during this crucial period were narrowed or abandoned in an atmosphere of stylish debate and selective formulations uncaring of (it seemed, finally, unaware of) the realities of human behaviour. Politicians in responsible positions urged what amounted to a Violence Eradication Scheme, as though Violence were a contagious disease curable by the elimination of infected bodies. Such politicians refused to consider the eradication of the causes of violence, and attempted to prevent discussion of such causes as 'unhelpful' and 'untimely'. It is probable that some of these considerations inspired the Irish electorate in 1977 to reject emphatically a Government grown so unrepresentative.

*

Butcher's Dozen was not written in response to the shooting of the thirteen dead in Derry. There are too many dead, on all sides, and it is no use pitting them hideously against one another. The poem was written in response to the Report of the Widgery Tribunal. In Lord Widgery's cold putting aside of truth, the *n*th in a historic series of expedient falsehoods — with Injustice literally wigged out as Justice — it was evident to me that we were suddenly very close to the operations of the evil real causes.

I couldn't write the same poem now. The pressures were special, the insult strongly felt, and the timing vital if the response was to matter, in all its kinetic impurity. Reaching for the nearest aid, I found the *aisling* form — that never

[57]

quite extinct Irish political verse-form — in a late, parodied guise: in the coarse energies and nightmare Tribunal of Merriman's *Midnight Court*. One changed one's standards, chose the doggerel route, and charged. . .

The poem was finished, printed and published within a week of the publication of the Widgery Report, and I believe it had the effect I wanted, 'unhelpful' though I am sure it was. It has been criticized on various grounds, some political: it did not put adequate emphasis on the Civil Rights campaign in the North; it did not lament the 'Protestant dead' — for which I was 'lowest of the low'; it did not mention the bigotry of the Catholic Church, or the Republic's censorship laws, or the law against the open sale of contraceptives; it was presumptuous of me to deal with the Northern issue at all — living in the Republic, I had not earned the right. It was criticised also for its motives: I had written it for publicity or for money. And it was criticised for its style. It offended many *a priori* assumptions as to poetic propriety of one kind or another, as to the place of poetry in public affairs, etc.; it was unwise in its directness of response; it was not poetry at all.

I have, in fact, a few regrets. I failed to fit in a reference to the culpable silence of the Catholic Church, North and South, in the face of Northern injustice during the long build-up to the current troubles. The poem doesn't bring out properly the price paid by the Northern majority for its long, grim dominance: its mediocrity, due to the exodus of its best intelligences. And it didn't occur to me then, what seems so obvious now, how easy and helpful it would have been, and still could be, for the Protestant minority in the South to have answered the hysterical sectarian warnings from the North about the horrors of possible Southern 'Rome Rule' — to ease this central sore merely by pointing to their own comfort and privileges, as a class, in the Republic.

*

On 6 October 1971, in the small town of Coolea in West Cork, a remarkable funeral took place. From every part and every element of the country many hundreds came to take their leave of Seán O Riada, a young man who had laid extraordinary hold on their emotions.

Seán O Riada was born in Cork in 1931 and died in a London hospital on 3 October 1971. There is general agreement that he was Ireland's foremost composer and musician, but there is some argument as to the main emphasis of his career.

Measured by orthodox standards, of the publication and performance of concert works, his achievement is small: half a dozen or so works for full orchestra, of varying scope, in advanced modern idiom and of striking quality; also a group of songs and some early piano pieces. The smallness of his output was not due to any lack of attention or praise from critics — indeed, to those accustomed to think only in terms of the orchestral or chamber ensemble, O Riada's refusal to fulfil their expectations seemed baffling and frustrating — a wilful refusal to fulfil a great potential.

For O Riada, however, the traditional 'European' relationship between the composer and a select audience appears from the beginning to have been uninspiring. His escape from it may come, in time, to be seen as his biggest achievement. It came about, not through any new devices, but through his revival of the old native relationship between Irish traditional music and the Irish community, and his renovation of it for the twentieth century. This enabled him to make the whole nation his audience for a time, and to affect it deeply, without abandoning musical standards.

The power to do this came from the modern means of mass communication, but also from a unique assembly of qualities in O Riada's material, in his national audience, and in himself. His primary material was Ireland's rich store of

traditional songs and dance tunes — the music of a sophis-
ticated tradition, which he was always at pains to distinguish
from folk music as usually understood. As he found it, this
music survived in relative purity only in certain remote Irish-
speaking areas of the country; elsewhere it had been debased
to a crude popular dance music. O Riada restored life and
nobility to it by his analytic ear for its essential melodic
excellence and by his great personal gift for presentation.
Avoiding the path of concert arrangements, he founded a
group of traditional musicians, the Ceoltóirí Chualann, in a
Dublin suburb, established over them an almost hypnotic
sway, and drew from them solo and ensemble performances
that astonished even themselves. The influence of this group
was felt immediately and widely, and transformed the world
of Irish traditional music for good.

But O Riada captured his widest audience with a feat of a
different kind. In the early sixties he was commissioned to
write the music for a documentary film Mise Eire *(I am*
Ireland); the film was to cover Ireland's struggle for political
freedom and to reach a climax with the Easter Rebellion of
1916. Fully aware of the reserves of national feeling such a
project might draw upon, O Riada went for his main theme
to Ireland's great emblematic song of lamentation and pride,
Róisín Dubh (The Black Rose); he virtually recreated it, and
wrung from it, in full Mahlerian and Sibelian harmonies,
every emotional possibility. It is a monument to his talent
that the result, while devastating the audience for whom it
was produced, remains a fine musical achievement.

Further concerts and recordings with the Ceoltóirí Chual-
ann, and other film music (some with the Ceoltóirí), accounted
for a great deal of O Riada's last ten years. His most recent
new work in music was the writing of a simple Mass for the
people of the Irish-speaking parish of Coolea, where he settled
down in 1964. This represented, of course, an even closer
relationship between music and the community, but it is
impossible to say what it would have come to, musically,

given time to develop — as it is impossible to say more of the country's loss by his early death than that it is great, and gravely felt.

T. K.

from *Eire/Ireland*, Bulletin of the Department of Foreign Affairs, Dublin : 14 January 1972.

*

Ceoltóirí Laighean number among them some of the very finest individual performers of Irish traditional music and song, as The Star of Munster *amply testifies. But they are even more important, as a group, for the ideal they represent, blending their talents in the lively expression of a noble tradition. The founding of Ceoltóirí Laighean in 1972 was a responsible act on the part of Eamon de Buitléar, who is trying to carry on what can be carried on of Seán O Riada's work.*

de Buitléar was an important member of O Riada's pioneering and influential group, Ceoltóirí Chualann, and remains committed to O Riada's aims — which went beyond the mere presentation of Irish music to a larger audience than it had ever had. He was in fact uniquely helpful to O Riada in the early 1960s in gathering the original musicians together. One of them was the Clare fiddler John Kelly who, with his knowledge of traditional tunes and local styles, became O Riada's guide into a virtually hidden world. John Kelly has keen memories of how traditional musicians were regarded up to that time, and as keen a sense of the dignity O Riada restored to them.

O Riada's decision to move from Dublin to Cúil Aodha in West Cork in 1964 put a certain strain on Ceoltóirí Chualann. They gathered for particular occasions but, for continuity and the fuller use of their talents, a number of them assembled together under the great piper Paddy Moloney as The Chieftains. *The Chieftains—the first offshoot of O Riada's work — have since developed their own style, using all O*

Riada's discoveries and inventions, and many of the tunes he revived (and composed), exploiting the music for sheer entertainment.

But for O Riada the music was as much a means as an end in itself, a means towards cultural integration; language, song and music fitted into, and fulfilling, a way of life. It is an ideal, requiring a very special community (at times, in Cúil Aodha, it seems close at hand . . .) and it is this ideal that brought Ceoltóirí Laighean into being — to realise, in music and song, whatever of it is possible.

T. K.

from the record sleeve for *The Star of Munster* — Gael-Linn : 1975.

*

This music is the last that Seán O Riada was concerned with. He had the tape with him in London during his last illness, and he seemed to cling to life with it. Listening with him to the unedited version, punctuated by his recorded voice in occasional vigorous comment, was a strange and painful experience.

In a full musical career, this record might seem an entertainment by the way, a charming personal flourish. As things happened, it must do duty as O Riada's farewell; it does so with elegance and appropriateness.

His more notable achievements in music have always involved others — the musicians and poets of the Gaelic past, his own Ceoltóirí, his adopted community in Coolea. These achievements, despite their communal aspect, were truly individual; like all art they stemmed from one tragically perishable talent. It is appropriate that O Riada's last offering should be not only traditional but a display of individual mastery.

T. K.

from the record sleeve note for *O Riada's Farewell* — Gael-Linn : 1972.

John Reidy was introduced to a number of us in Dublin in 1951, in the students' restaurant in 86 St. Stephen's Green. He had finished his degree in music in University College, Cork, and was in Dublin for an interview. He was pale and thin, and playful under scrutiny. He laid claim to absolute pitch and, by suggestion, to absolute knowledge in musical matters. Two musicians in the company tested him and swiftly revealed their limitations. His use of a Latin quotation was matched by another, but he shook off pursuit with something in Greek that sounded fluent and convincing. His French sounded excellent; it certainly impressed two girls who were taking their M.A. in French. Someone from Trim was trying to define existentialism; he set the definition right. Likewise with progressive jazz: he was dogmatic about Jerry Mulligan and George Shearing. He had played the jazz piano himself, professionally. . .

I was working in the Department of Finance at the time. I must have been on leave that day, because I remember sitting on with Reidy when the others had left, dabbing out butts in a wet saucer. I forget most of what we talked about, but I remember enjoying his company and being drawn to him by the recognition that our minds shared an odd blend of rigour and squalor. We had earlier dismissed without much discussion the whole mentality of the 'L & H' — the Literary and Historical Society at U.C.D. : all syllogisms, debating brilliance and commanding mannerisms. Now we were pleased to discover a common interest in science fiction. We were in agreement on the merits of Hal Clements, whose *Mission of Gravity* was just then appearing in serial form in *Astounding*. Reidy had read Olaf Stapledon and we agreed on his importance.

We walked that evening by the canal and along the South Circular Road toward Dolphin's Barn, where he confessed that he believed in ghosts — he had actually heard one approaching him, opening and closing door after door, down the corridors of a deserted hotel in Valentia. I told him that

[63]

I believed in God, and he was interested but puzzled. He went back to Cork next day.

He had been in Dublin trying for a job as Assistant Director of Music in Radio Eireann. He was soon notified that he had been successful and he wrote to say he was coming to Dublin to look for a place to live. Early one afternoon I was talking to a visitor in the lobby of the Department of Finance in Merrion Street, at the side window overlooking the grounds of the Natural History Museum. Looking out on the summer sunshine, I noticed that people going in the direction of Clare Street were staring at something. An extraordinary, sombre figure came into view : it was Reidy, with death-white face, in a long black tight overcoat, with black umbrella, black beret, gloves and scarf. He turned in at the Department steps and I watched him through the glass partition being ushered into the waiting room, where he sat erect and expressionless on the edge of the seat, the umbrella held upright in front of him. The porter nodded to me, smiling unsurely.

He had returned, and he was here to ask if he might stay in Baggot Street with me while the search for his own place proceeded. He went off to meet some people from Radio Eireann, and didn't arrive at the flat until very late. He slept on the floor, and was still asleep when I left for the office next morning. At lunchtime, when I looked in, he was beginning to stir. He seemed to expect breakfast. I left him to fend for himself and didn't see him until late that evening. He had met a few people from Radio Eireann and had done nothing about finding a place. He would give up to-morrow to that.

We listened to some records on a record player I was buying — a real extravagance. The sounds were clean and wonderful : Bach's cello suites, the *Orgelbuechlein* . . . a refreshing rigour. But also Sibelius's Second Symphony, with the long excitations and glittering elephantine climax of the finale. . .

We talked until very late, in various accents. Reidy was very good at American, and also at a glutinous Balkan voice.

He had a great store of good dirty stories. He retired to the floor and we intoned Wordsworth's sonnet *Upon Westminster Bridge* antiphonally, in BBC voices.

Next morning he slept late again. As I left for the Department I pulled the curtains back to let in the light. I didn't call in at lunch time and when I came home at five o'clock he was gone. I worked a little and made a pot of tea, and sat reading. He came in late and said he had had no luck with the search; no one he met knew anything about an available place. I asked had he looked at the small ads in the newspapers. He hadn't, but he would try the next day.

It lasted a week. One night, as he hovered over my bookshelves, I ran my eye down the advertisements in the evening paper and picked out an item almost at random. It was in Lower Mount Street, on the corner facing Clanwilliam House. It was fairly expensive for what it was (a dark rat-trap partitioned off a back landing). I told him it was a rare opportunity, so central, not to be missed. He moved in at once.

He too bought a record player. He had access to Radio Eireann's entire record library and brought many records home with him. I remember the elaborate, opulent close of *Der Rosenkavalier* filling the mean little space: the unmade single bed, the dusty electric fire glowing in the grate, spattered with butts, Reidy's narrow, unfocussed face intent in the dark like an animal. I heard Mahler there for the first time. Reidy played *Das Lied von der Erde* again and again. And Jerry Mulligan, and George Shearing.

When it was time for regression, and squallor came uppermost, we would cruise the dark streets looking for a little harmless evil, ineffectual, like a pair of ill-matched adolescents. We sat drinking coffee late one night in a gaunt night-place on the quays. The air was smoky, the board floor bare and unswept, the atmosphere cavernous and ugly. Someone was 'vamping' at the piano and Reidy complained so much I suggested he do something about it. He was a moderately good player but always very reluctant, because he liked to grow his fingernails very long, and they scraped when he played. But the idea of the gesture tempted him. He went up to the pianist and asked to play, then sat down and tore off the tops of his nails and played for a quarter of an hour to the admiration of the surrounding tables.

The first drunken evening I recall was spent with some journalists in a pub called *The Kind Ladies*, a dreary den in a street of warehouses somewhere behind Amiens Street. We were a pair of simple and lonely seamen from the Baltic, and were made welcome as such. We made monosyllabic attempts at communication with the inhabitants, in soft expletives, and there was a lot of laughter. The circular table was crowded with glasses and opened bottles; dregs and floating ash washed about.

He married shortly after, and he and Ruth stayed in a flat in Merrion Square, which gave them access to the Square itself, then closed to the public. He assembled a model airplane and flew it there, chasing it across the unkempt grass in his long open black overcoat, as it crashed again and again until it could fly no more.

Sometimes he would talk obsessively about his musical plans. There were to be a number of orchestral suites that he called 'nomoi', one in particular to be a huge choral work using choruses from Sophocles. I knew his working method and his short attention span, and would have laid odds against these works being completed. But they all were, sooner or later.

The first pieces to emerge were for piano. They were very short, and made up of tiny units. He played one at a lunch-time concert in Trinity College. It had a series of glissandi at one point running up the entire keyboard : there were at least half a dozen of these one after the other, identical, and separated by dead rests. The sparse audience could scarcely believe its ears. About the same time he gave a radio talk in his British accent. This too was excruciating. At the time he was gruffly determined about it, but he destroyed the recording afterwards and all evidence of the episode, and winced at any mention of it. He was also starting to write a few settings of Irish airs, very direct and 'intelligent'. I believe there is absolute intelligence, as there is absolute pitch, and that Reidy had it. But the playfulness of his mind had not begun to find vent in his work.

*

In 1959 we arranged for our two young families to go together on holidays to Ballyferriter in West Kerry. A former teacher of Reidy's, Father Tadhg O Murchadha, had built a summer school in An Gráig and we could stay there until the students came.

I was delayed in Dublin for a week. At the end of the week I got the train to Tralee, then a bus to Dingle, where Reidy was waiting to take me on the last stage to An Gráig. He was very excited : he had found great singers and music, Jerry Flaherty and Seán de Hóra, in Kruger Kavanagh's pub in Dunquin, and we must go and hear them straight away.

The porch of Kruger's was full of upturned barrels with a few people sitting on them. The interior of the shop was dark and cool, murmurous, and filled with presences. Reidy went up to the bar and bought drinks for everyone in the shop and chatted them all, using a very sketchy Irish but doing so unabashed, mimicking fluency. It was clear he had established himself as a character over the past week, and not only in the realm of pub talk : he was committing himself to fairly serious schemes, to using his influence in Dublin to get a fishmeal plant for the district, and grants for greenhouses for commercial tomato growing.

A voice from a dark corner near the fireplace began to sing. The song was *Casadh an tSúgáin* and the singer Jerry Flaherty. I had heard the *sean nós*, or old style, of traditional singing before, without being attracted by the raw Oriental tonalities or the nasalised, strangulated delivery. For whatever reasons, the effect was different now. Nothing intervened

[67]

between the song and its expression. The singer managed many difficult things, but the result was to focus attention on the song, not on the performance or on the quality of the voice. It was a special voice, adapted (like a reptile or an insect) to its function. Mere beauty of tone would have distracted, attracting attention for its own sake. And the singer's act of communication was thoroughly completed by his audience. They sat erect and listened, lifted their glasses and drank, and murmured phrases of appreciation. When the song ended there was a slight increase in the volume of general approbation but very little fuss. Something had been accomplished, and the entities which had combined to accomplish it separated and began to chat, in the smells of fish, rope, tobacco and porter.

I was introduced and welcomed. I met the singer, Jerry Flaherty, most courteous, but untalkative. He was a fisherman and farmer like most of the local people, with a wide-cheeked lipless face like a cobra, and black slit eyes shaded under his cap. I met his friend Seán de Hóra also, small and erect-necked, most correct and polite. And Kruger Kavanagh himself, the publican, with his square clipped head, and his elbow on the counter, emphatic and confiding. ('Schubert? I knew Schubert. A great man. I worked with him in America: Boston and Philadelphia and Springfield, Massachussetts. I went ahead to the next town and did the publicity for all his concerts.') He turned to get a bottle, pivoting on his bent little finger. His heavy body moved independently in the receptacle of his great frieze trousers.

Outside, the Blasket Islands crouched on the water. We walked back toward An Gráig. As the road rounded a headland of scraggy shale the scene opened toward Ballyferriter, on a landscape of immense depth and volume, like nothing I had ever seen before. On the right, the flank of Croagh-marhin receded for miles. To the left, the fields sloped down to the bay at Clochar; foam like ragged lace crawled and gleamed rangerously in the Blasket Sound, where remnants of the Armada still lie wrecked. In the centre, a range of headlands poured westward out to the ocean like huge breakers; on one of them, above a low cliff, were the ruins of the poet Piaras Feiritéar's castle. In the distance Mount Brandon closed the scene, the holy mountain of Saint Brendan the Navigator, with a narrow creek somewhere at its base, An Cuas, where his great voyage began to the unknown Western world. Dead centre in this prospect, under a sky full of oceanic movement, at the foot of an extraordinary little hill crested with a cock's comb of shattered rock, was our home : An tAthair Tadhg's hostel, a two-story concrete box starting up naked out of the ground, sharp-gabled and drain-piped.

We spent a couple of weeks there, the two families passing their time in separate ways. Reidy was usually in Kruger's, where he was beginning to pace his pints with glasses of Paddy or vodka. He and I went shrimping together a lot of the time, catching the tiny monsters singly with the childrens' pinkeen nets, the little grey phantoms cloudily 'cycling' (as Reidy called it) alongside the dark boatslip at Smerwyck. I enjoyed the long stress-free days and read science fiction and Wodehouse and some of the Irish books lying about the hostel. There were three issues of the folklore journal *Béaloideas*, from the 1930s, containing a long work by An Seabhac on the place-names of the Dingle peninsula. Reidy and I were fascinated by this, and 'did' the places between Dunquin and Ballyferriter. I had encountered An Seabhac in school, as the author of *Jimín Máire Thaidhg*, simple funny stories of a young boy's growing up in the Gaeltacht at the turn of the century. Now 'The Hawk' took on new flesh : an enthusiast, a teacher and researcher, heroic with notebook and bicycle clips, ranging the landscape I could feel coming to life around us.

For Reidy it was all a swift liberation, as he drove off toward Kruger's in Dunquin or O Catháin's in Ballyferriter, bustling with business, chatting and joking with the people,

[69]

exchanging songs and stories, charming and impressing them, pitching himself forward into the language with predatory energy in a spate of new ideas. As we threw ourselves down again on the slip at Smerwyck, our heads over the edge, looking into the dark water, the childrens' nets dipping toward their prey on their long canes, he turned and said : 'I feel as if I have never done anything else in my life.'

Every night there was music and singing somewhere. And always drink. We threw a party in the hostel at the end of our stay. 'Iron lungs' full of stout stood on trestles in a shed, benches were arranged along the walls, Seán de Hóra played his melodeon in the corner. It went on until almost dawn : the last to leave were de Hóra and Jerry Flaherty, walking homeward together toward Clochar in their familiar setting of slopes and headlands, luminous growling ocean and apocalyptic Western sky.

We didn't see them again until the following September, when they came to see the final at Croke Park and to make a few trial recordings for Gael-Linn. In Reidy's house in Galloping Green they spoke of the good fishing season that was just starting : after years elsewhere the big mackerel shoals had come back and they were anxious to get home and make the most of it. The next Sunday I picked up the paper and saw a photograph of an upturned black skin-boat on the quay at Dingle, and a great heap of mackerel, still tangled in the torn net. Jerry Flaherty and two others were missing; they were never found. Two of his songs had been recorded, one — *An Seanduine* — was issued by Gael-Linn as a single 78; the other — *Casadh an tSúgáin* — was unsatisfactory in some way and never issued.

Reidy's liberation continued. He pursued the schemes and the grants, and I believe that some of his ideas did lead to something. But a profounder consequence of our holiday, of course, was his unabated new drive toward Irish music. It was a recovery, in fact : he had only to become conscious of it to realise that he was already in possession of it, from the time

[70]

he played the traditional fiddle as a young boy growing up in Bruff, County Limerick, where his father had been a police sergeant. He was rapidly setting something free in himself, with all the intelligence and playfulness of which he was capable.

*

In *A Selected Life*, in the first part of section (ii), the circumstances are as 'given' : things noted during a short walk away from the crowds in the O Riada household on the morning of the funeral — rain, the crow, the coarse bell sounding across open country. It was only afterwards that I was struck by the parallels with the well-known lines from 'Marbhna Oiliféir Grás' by Seán mac Bháitéir Breathnach :

> Tá cling na marbh leis an ngaoith,
> Monuar! is teachta bróin dúinn í!
> Tá an fiach dubh le glór garbh
> Ag fógradh uaire an duine mhairbh.
>
> (The clang for the dead is on the wind,
> our messenger of grief, alas!
> The raven with a rough voice
> announces the dead man's hour.)

Parts of *A Selected Life* are saturated in alcohol. . . O Riada was a reasonably moderate drinker until his late twenties, but then his metabolism seemed to accelerate, and he drank heavily. I have known others, and know some still, who could drink more than he did, but I have never known anyone with the same destructive affinity for alcohol. In the last ten years of his life he aged quickly, so that in his middle thirties he looked to be about sixty. One night, when he was in hospital in London, I brought something he had asked for earlier in the day : the night nurse let me in with great reluctance, and the warning : 'Remember, he is a very old man.'

The genesis of *Vertical Man* is the strangest of any poem I have written. The September after O Riada's death I was back in Philadelphia after more than a year's absence in Dublin. I brought O Riada's death mask with me, and a cast of his left hand. A few weeks after my return, after a day spent working on poems from a long sequence and on *The Good Fight*, I started unpacking old books and records in my apartment. While I dusted them and arranged them in their places I played a few records. I came upon the record *Vertical Man*, with O Riada's photograph on the sleeve, sitting in his waistcoat, with cigar, and quizzical face averted, dangling a lay figure in front of him with surreptitious obscenity. I propped the record sleeve against the bookcase, under the death mask and the hand, making a little altar. I finished the tidying, and picked out *Das Lied von der Erde*. I poured a glass of Bourbon and stood proposing a toast to the picture, the death mask and the hand. Out in the city darkness there was a sudden terrifying amplified screaming. I filled with panic — being still unaccustomed, after my long absence, to the alarums of the fire station around the corner in Market Street. I relaxed and drank, and then O Riada's presence was in the room; for an extraordinary moment we drank together. Then the presence went off into the darkness. It was a definite farewell. It is the only experience of the kind I have had, and it occurred on the first anniversary of O Riada's death.

On the second and third pages of the poem offerings are being made to the ghost, in propitiation : two sentences from Plato's *The Laws*, from among the drafts of *The Good Fight*, and the 'plot' of the long sequence I had been working on during the day.

The closing section of *Vertical Man*, apart from the last three quatrains, is based on the poem used by Gustav Mahler

in the opening movement of *Das Lied von der Erde*. The text
of the poem, *Das Trinklied vom Jammer der Erde* by Hans
Bethge, is as follows :

Schon winkt der Wein im gold'nen Pokale,
Doch trink noch nicht, erst sing ich euch ein Lied !
Das Lied vom Kummer soll auflachend
In die Seele euch klingen. Wenn der Kummer naht,
Liegen wüst die Gärten der Seele,
Welkt hin und stirbt die Freude, der Gesang.
Dunkel ist das Leben, ist der Tod.

Herr dieses Hauses !
Dein Keller birgt die Fülle des goldenen Weins !
Hier diese Laute nenn ich mein !
Die Laute schlagen und die Gläser leeren,
Das sind die Dinge, die zusammenpassen.
Ein voller Becher Wein zur rechten Zeit
Ist mehr wert als alle Reiche dieser Erde.
Dunkel ist das Leben, ist der Tod.

Das Firmament blaut ewig, und die Erde
Wird lange feststehn und aufblühn im Lenz.
Du aber, Mensch, wie lange lebst denn du?
Nicht hundert Jahre darfst du dich ergötzen
An all dem morschen Tande dieser Erde !

Seht dort hinab !
Im Mondschein auf den Gräbern hockt
Eine wild-gespenstiche Gestalt. Ein Aff ist's !
Hört ihr, wie sein Heulen hinausgellt
In den süssen Duft des Lebens !
Jetzt nehmt den Wein ! Jetzt ist es Zeit, Genossen !
Leert eure goldnen Becher zu Grund !
Dunkel ist das Leben, ist der Tod.

[73]

Vertical Man is the title chosen by Seán O Riada for the Claddagh Records recording of a number of his songs and the orchestral *Hercules Dux Ferrariae*. It appears to have been taken from the following dedicatory verse in W. H. Auden's *Poems* (1930):

To Christopher Isherwood

Let us honour if we can
The vertical man
Though we value none
But the horizontal one.

*

THE GOOD FIGHT

With this fifteenth death many things died, foolish expectations and assumptions, as it now seems. I began the poem soon after Kennedy's assassination — with how many other poems written for a while, as people roamed the nights to relieve themselves of obscure pressures. But the poem jammed and allowed time for the foolishness to digest. A great deal of foreign matter was lifted from it, and developed into a separate poem, *Worker in Mirror, at His Bench*.

In section I the speeches are made up partly of quotations from various Kennedy speeches, interviews and articles. The opening of the first speech, on page 38, is taken from a contemporary song, 'The New Frontier'; there are also sentences from Plato's *The Republic*. The italicised passages on pages 37, 40 and 41 consist mainly of quotations from Plato's *The Republic* and *The Laws*.

Elsewhere in section I and in section III individual images and phrases are taken from *The Making of the President 1960* by Theodore H. White (New York, 1961), *The Kennedy Promise* by Henry Fairlie (London, 1973), and contemporary news reports.

In section II part of the psychological argument is borrowed from 'The Silence of Oswald', an article by John Clellon Holmes in *Playboy*, November 1965. The article assumes Oswald's guilt in the assassination, and this assumption is accepted for the purpose in hand. Many of the images, and two short passages *verbatim* (the suicide vision and the final note) are taken from Oswald's own 'Historic Diary'. The passages in bold type towards the end of the section are selected, again, from Plato.